MW00439780

Twilight of the Wolves

by Jason Lublinski
illustrated by Jerry Tiritilli

Editorial Offices: Glenview, Illinois • Parsippany, New Jersey • New York, New York
Sales Offices: Needham, Massachusetts • Duluth, Georgia • Glenview, Illinois
Coppell, Texas • Ontario, California • Mesa, Arizona

Every effort has been made to secure permission and provide appropriate credit for photographic material. The publisher deeply regrets any omission and pledges to correct errors called to its attention in subsequent editions.

Unless otherwise acknowledged, all photographs are the property of Scott Foresman, a division of Pearson Education.

Illustrations by Jerry Tiritilli

ISBN: 0-328-13594-1

Copyright © Pearson Education, Inc.

All Rights Reserved. Printed in the United States of America. This publication is protected by Copyright, and permission should be obtained from the publisher prior to any prohibited reproduction, storage in a retrieval system, or transmission in any form by any means, electronic, mechanical, photocopying, recording, or likewise. For information regarding permission(s), write to: Permissions Department, Scott Foresman, 1900 East Lake Avenue, Glenview, Illinois 60025.

5 6 7 8 9 10 V0G1 14 13 12 11 10 09 08 07

Chapter One: Daggerut's Tale

I had lived in the forest near Iverrut, the wide river, for many, many lunar cycles before the humans came.

My name is Ankrut. I am a large gray wolf, and I was, for many years, the Thonuk, chieftain of my tribe. My wife, whom I love dearly, is called Bona. Together, we have seven children, all of whom are now adults with families of their own.

However, none of them were more than pups when the humans first arrived in our part of the world, which I suppose you would call "Oregon," in your human-speak.

We had heard the rumors long before the humans came, of course. Other wolves from tribes that lived farther to the east would sometimes come and visit us, staying for a day, or perhaps for many days. Most of them would tell us stories about humans that made the fur upon our backs grow stiff with fright.

The tales varied greatly, depending upon the teller. But there were many common elements: Humans were invariably described as hunters, predators, and warriors.

They used strange and elaborate weapons we had never heard of before. And they had, we were told, no great love for wolves.

I can remember one storyteller in particular. He was an old, shaggy wolf of the Yongis tribe. He came to us roughly a year before the humans arrived, and he stayed with us for about a week.

His name was Daggerut. Although aged, he still cut an imposing figure. His coat was black and speckled with fine silver hairs that made him look quite dignified.

He had been the chieftain of the Yongis until the humans came. Now, he told us sadly, there was no more Yongis tribe to be chieftain of.

"No tribe?" my youngest son, Ceckut, asked him, surprised.

Daggerut shook his head grimly. "None at all."

"I don't understand," piped up my daughter Osa.

"They drove us out," Daggerut explained. "You see, the humans decided that they liked our land. They liked it so much that they wanted to make it their own."

"They conquered your land?" asked Ceckut.

Daggerut gave a dry chuckle at this.

"If that is the way you choose to phrase it," he said. "They took over our land and hunted us down when we got in their way."

When he said this, many of my wolves eyed one another with fear.

"They have strange, terrible weapons," Daggerut continued. "Sticks that they hold in both hands. The sticks spit shrieking things that fly through the air and wound you. Maybe even . . ."

He did not have to finish the sentence. Much of my tribe shivered at the thought of these awful human-sticks.

"What became of the rest of your pack?" I asked.

"They have scattered throughout the Great Forest," he replied grimly. "Some have traveled west, toward the Mother Ocean. Others have gone north. With its members running off in all directions, the Yongis tribe survives only in my memories."

My tribemates looked horrified that such a great and powerful tribe could simply cease to exist. After all, the Yongis had long been the fiercest warriors of wolfkind. They were both brave and strong, yet they were still honorable in combat. They never harmed the weak or wounded, and pups were not permitted to go into battle until they had grown and proven themselves.

"Why do these humans drive our kind away?" Bona asked Daggerut.

"I wish I could say," he replied. "But I do not know. They do not talk with us, for they do not know wolf-speak. They have a language of their own, but it is most strange."

"Is there no way to reason with these humans, then?" I interjected. "If not through speech, then through some other form of communication?"

Although I could not show my true emotions to my tribe, I was beginning to panic at the thought of these rowdy humans and their rough, alien ways.

"If there is," responded Daggerut, "then I have yet to learn of it."

"They would not listen?" I persisted.

"They cannot listen," Daggerut corrected me. "It is not their way. I observed the humans, and I saw that they did not listen to any of the other creatures of the woodland, either. They do not even try to understand. I have never once seen a human attempt to learn another creature's language. For some reason, they seem content with their ignorance and their isolation."

Daggerut's words disturbed me. I lay awake most of the night thinking about what he had said. As the leader of my tribe, it was my responsibility to learn all I could of this new threat.

The next morning, I decided to take Daggerut aside in order to speak with him privately.

"Walk with me a while," I said. "I will show you a peaceful spot where fresh water flows through the forest."

"Yes, I would like that," he said, and he followed me deep into the woods.

"You are a wise and fair chieftain, Daggerut," I said, as we trotted along together on a dirt path dappled by sunlight shining through the trees.

"Was," he replied, with an ironic smile. "I was a wise and fair chieftain, Ankrut. I am no longer a chieftain."

"These things do not change, my friend," I told him. "With or without a tribe, you are a chieftain and will always remain one."

"Well," he said, with a shrug, "I am pleased that you think so, at any rate."

We arrived at a clearing, where a small stream trickled across the rocks. We paused to lap up some of the water that flowed by.

There was a long pause as we sat by the river.

"I assume," said Daggerut, "that you did not bring me here merely to allow me to partake of this fine water."

"I wanted to ask you something, Daggerut," I admitted.

"Ask, then," responded the older wolf.

I stopped and looked at him for a moment. It saddened me to see how lost and shabby this once-great warrior now appeared. "Did you fight?" I asked him. "When the humans came to drive you out, did you fight?"

Daggerut smiled at me, his sharp fangs gleaming in the early morning sunlight.

"Oh, yes," he replied, sounding more tired than before. "We fought. Did you ever doubt it?"

I shook my head. I had never thought that they would surrender what was rightly theirs without a battle.

Daggerut also shook his great shaggy head sadly. "It did no good," he said. "We have been defeated before, of course. No tribe can win every battle. But we had never before been beaten so easily. There was hardly any contest; I can barely even call it a proper battle."

He shook his head again and frowned at me.

"Listen to me carefully, Ankrut," he said. "If the humans come, and if they decide that they want your home, as well—"

"I will do as you did," I interrupted. "We are not great warriors like the Yongis, but we are not cowards, either. If the humans try to take what is ours, we will fight."

"No!" hissed Daggerut, startling me with the earnestness of his reaction. "That is precisely what you must not do!"

"Not fight?" I asked him, bewildered. Never before would I have expected the chieftain of the Yongis tribe to argue against the necessity of warfare.

"You must not!" he insisted, his eyes flashing. "I understand why you think you should, Ankrut. You are a good Thonuk, and as such, you imagine that it would be dishonorable to give up without a fight."

"It *would* be dishonorable," I said, my eyes narrowing.

"Don't be a fool!" Daggerut hissed again, surprising me. "Pride means little compared to life. When the humans came, I thought fighting was the only answer. I saw that they intended to drive us away, and I felt that I was obligated to take a stand against them. But it was the worst mistake that I ever made."

"A mistake?" I asked.

"Oh, yes, a terrible mistake," he repeated. "Many of my best wolves died. The humans beat us with little effort on their part. I told you about their weapon-sticks last night. Let me assure you, these sticks are dangerous."

The thought that humans might have access to such dangerous tools chilled me to the bone. How could we possibly take a stand against them?

"The funny thing," Daggerut continued, "is that when alone, a human is much weaker than a wolf. He is neither swift nor agile, and he lacks sharp claws and teeth.

"But once they group together and use their sticks, they are unbeatable," Daggerut lamented. "The sticks make awful noises and can kill a wolf with ease. With stick in hand, a human becomes as fierce as a mountain lion. It is sheer insanity to oppose them."

"We have often fought in times when victory seemed unlikely," I said stubbornly.

"Unlikely, yes," Daggerut allowed. "But never impossible. Let me assure you, victory over the humans *is* impossible. I learned the hard way. Because of my foolish warrior's pride, many of my tribemates died."

"It was not your fault," I said.

"Then whose was it?" he shot back. "Yes, it was my fault. I am to blame. If I had had half a brain, I would have packed up my tribe in the dead of night and fled. I would have traveled far, far away.

"But I didn't," he continued. "I fought, and I lost. My tribe was destroyed. Those who did not die on the field of battle were so terrified that they ran off in all directions. I shall never see them again. That is my punishment for my poor leadership."

"You were a great leader," I insisted.

"No, I was not," replied Daggerut. "But, at the very least, I hope that you will be able to learn from my mistakes."

When he left a few days later to make his aimless way westward, I could feel all hope for my tribe drifting away with him. Disappearing into the forest, and bound for a place far away from here, Daggerut and those hopes were soon gone from my sight.

Still, I had to be strong. After all, I was Thonuk, and I had a responsibility to do all that I could to protect my tribe and to preserve our home.

But I had no idea what I could do. I could only hope the humans would never want our land.

Chapter Two: Wolf Meets Human

We stewed in our uncertainty, nervous and high-strung, for the remainder of the year. The tension around my tribe was so thick it seemed tangible as it hung in the air around us. No wolf felt quite at ease in those days.

We wondered what humans looked like. Did they resemble us, with shaggy coats, long snouts, and four legs? Or were they odder creatures altogether? Did they tower overhead, like the trees of the forest? Were they small but fierce, like the stinging wasp? Were they something we could not imagine at all?

One day, in the spring of what you would know as the year 1840, we finally found out. Day had scarcely dawned when my son Barrut came lunging into the tribal grounds, eyes aflame with a sort of terrified, yet elated, curiosity.

"I've seen them!" he shouted to all willing to listen, which was, of course, all of us. "Humans! Coming this way!"

"Humans!" The murmur traveled through the pack like rain-ripples spreading across a pond.

In a few moments, we were transformed from a normal wolf tribe, sleepily contemplating the prospect of a morning hunt, to a mass of wide-eyed, nervously twitching beasts.

Every member of the tribe wanted to see the humans, so strong was our shared curiosity. But I knew that this was not a good idea.

It would not do for the humans to see the tribe in its entirety. There was a chance that they would view us as an approaching army and lash out at us.

However, I reasoned, if I were to assemble a small party of my most trusted lieutenants, we might be able to sneak over and take a quiet look at the humans, and know something of our new friends, or enemies. So, I selected four of the most trustworthy wolves in the tribe: Tagrut, Patrut, Spinnut, and Tolla.

Together, we set out to investigate the arrival of the humans. We crossed a small stream and trotted through the sun-dappled undergrowth of the forest. Anticipation, mixed with excitement and also fear, made the trek feel longer than it was.

We were padding silently across a stony hilltop when we stopped short. There, in a clearing beneath us, we caught our first glimpse of humankind.

I will admit, the humans looked nothing like what I had expected. They were tall and pale with ridiculously skinny bodies. They stood on two legs and had far too little hair on their bodies. The only hair I could see sat on the tops of their heads.

"So little hair," mused Tolla, quietly. "Perhaps they're a kind of bird? Do they have feathers?"

Tagrut and Patrut laughed softly at her joke. But I, for one, was in no mood to laugh. There were about ten humans in the clearing below us, both male and female.

Oddly, the male and female humans looked very different from one another. Most notably, the females had long, flowing hair on their heads, which I found to be quite beautiful and almost wolflike. They had it tied up in strange patterns around their heads or left it to trail down their backs.

Even more oddly, the humans were covered in strange hanging cloths, from head to foot. The idea of wearing something upon your body, other than a coat of fur that was a part of you, seemed truly bizarre and alien to me.

"Look!" whispered Spinnut, pointing with his muzzle. "What is that thing?"

I looked in the direction he was pointing and saw an object quite unlike anything I'd ever seen before. Much time has passed since that day. Now, of course, I know that the object I was looking at was a covered wagon, the vehicle that the humans had arrived in. A team of exhausted horses stood nearby, whinnying and shaking off the dust of the trail, which had coated their flanks and matted their hair.

At the time, of course, I recognized neither wagon nor horses. The contraption was strange to me, and the four-legged animals were not of a breed that I recognized.

"I don't know," I told Spinnut. "I've never seen such things."

Then I noticed something truly astounding. There was a fire blazing, right there in the middle of the human camp! Even more astonishing was the fact that the humans didn't seem to mind. On the contrary, they scarcely gave the blaze a single glance.

The only time we wolves had encountered fire before was during storms, when the great forked lightning came down from the sky and struck the trees of the forest. Wherever the lightning struck, fierce fires would kindle. Wolves knew enough to fear fire, and we always fled.

Apparently, however, humans did not have as much sense as wolves. Not only were they not afraid of the fire, but, I realized, they were foolishly trying to use it to their own advantage.

As I stared, unbelieving, a human pierced a thick piece of meat with a long, sharp stick, and then held it out over the fire.

"What is he doing?" asked Spinnut. "Does he want to set himself ablaze? Is he mad?"

"I don't know," I responded, baffled by these strange actions.

The odd thing was nothing bad seemed to be happening to the human. In fact, a strangely pleasant smell was now rising from the meat. We wolves eat little but meat, day in and day out, but I had never smelled meat that gave off an aroma like this before.

"That smells wonderful," said Tolla.

"Heavenly," agreed Patrut.

"I don't understand what they are doing," I whispered. "It seems as if the human uses the fire to change the meat. To make it better."

"How could that be?" asked Tagrut. "Fire doesn't make things better, it just burns them to ash."

After another few moments, the human tore a large chunk off the piece of meat and began chewing on it. He made a series of noises that seemed to indicate that he was quite pleased with the taste. If it tasted as good as it smelled, I could scarcely blame him.

"Perhaps we can befriend the humans," Patrut said. "Then they can teach us how to make meat smell so delicious."

"Perhaps," I agreed, with a smile. Patrut was one of my best wolves, but he often thought with his stomach rather than his brain.

"Listen," Tagrut said to me, lowering his voice even further. "Do you see those strange thin-legged animals?"

He pointed to the horses with his long snout. I nodded.

"I'd like to go over and try talking to one," he said. "Perhaps it will tell us more about these humans."

"It's a risk," I said. "Perhaps the thin-legs are an ally of the humans. Perhaps they will sound an alarm."

"I know," said Tagrut. "Still, I would like to try. With your permission, sir."

I thought for a moment, then shrugged my shoulders.

"Yes, you have my permission, Tagrut," I said. "But please be careful. Be polite to the thin-legs, and do not insult them."

"Yes, yes, yes," snorted Tagrut. "I will be the perfect diplomat." And with that he took off.

"I don't like it," said Spinnut. "It's not a good idea. We know nothing about the thin-legs. They may be vicious."

"If they are," I said, "they do a fine job of concealing it. No, Spinnut, I do not think that the thin-legs are a threat in and of themselves. I am more concerned that they will alert the humans to our presence here."

"And is that not a dangerous possibility?" Spinnut asked.

"I trust Tagrut," I replied. "If the situation becomes dangerous, he will alert us, and we will retreat before anything happens."

Spinnut shrugged. I had not convinced him that I had made the right decision in allowing Tagrut to carry out his mission. Still, I was Thonuk, and Spinnut was my lieutenant: He had no choice but to defer to me in this matter.

So, we hunkered down and waited for Tagrut to return. Time seemed to slow to a crawl. But what could we do? Until Tagrut returned, we could not leave the human camp.

After what seemed like an eternity, but was probably only a few minutes, Tagrut came slinking back to our position.

"Well," he said, looking disgusted, "that was certainly useless."

"Was it?" I asked.

"Worse than useless," he snarled. "The thin-legs are idiots. They know some wolf-speak, but their accents are terrible. It's almost impossible to understand a single word that they say!"

"What did they say?" asked Tolla.

"I kept on asking this one old thin-legs about the humans," Tagrut replied, "and he kept saying, 'Zis apple iz SO goot!' That's all he said, over and over again! So, I guess, now we know that the old thin-legs likes the apple he's eating. But that's about all we know."

"Well, it could have been worse," I said. "At least the thin-legs didn't sound the alarm."

I glanced back down at the human camp. Now, several more humans were using the fire to change the smell of their meat.

"A useful technique," I murmured. "Perhaps we can learn from the humans, after all."

"If they are willing to teach it to us," said Tolla. "Which is not a sure thing, by any means."

"I'm not without hope," I admitted. Despite my final, grim conversation with Daggerut, I had never given up on the possibility that we could befriend the humans.

I turned back to the human camp and scrutinized it once again. I had to admit, Daggerut was right. Humans seemed to be oddly weak creatures. At least in the physical sense. They moved so awkwardly. I couldn't imagine how they could possibly survive out in the wilderness.

Perhaps they couldn't. Perhaps that was why they disliked us: They envied our survival skills. Because, you see, wolves are nothing if not adaptable. We are, in fact, natural-born survivalists.

I was still afraid of the humans and confused by their strangeness. But, I confess, I also found them to be quite fascinating. I couldn't stop watching them. They were so different from any other creature that I'd ever encountered before.

I watched them slowly eat the meat that they'd placed near the fire. If humankind had truly learned how to exploit the power of fire, how mighty they must be!

As we watched, something strange and unexpected began to occur in the human camp.

I was surprised to see one human male suddenly seize the hands of a female and begin romping around, grinning and making an odd musical noise in his throat. Although the ways of the humans were strange to me, I recognized the movements for what they were: a dance. Wolves know much about dancing; it is our most sacred ritual.

As I watched the two humans dance, both smiling, a sudden feeling of hope rose within me. If humans understood the power, the majesty of dancing, perhaps they were not so strange after all. If they shared this ritual with wolves, then perhaps we might be able to communicate with them.

And so I allowed myself to be seen. I stepped forward, to the very crest of the stony hilltop high above the humans, and howled once to attract their attention.

Immediately, the humans froze in their tracks. All eyes turned to me.

I began to dance. I danced the wolf-dance of Ut-Nizak, one of our most sacred dances, a dance of friendship and welcome.

It is a very complicated dance and not easy to describe to the one who does not know it. Suffice it to say that it involves leaps and twists, counterclockwise rotations, and a number of ceremonial paw-waves. Would they see and understand, and return the gesture?

To my dismay, the humans did not understand the dance. They watched for a while, eyes empty, as if baffled by my actions. Then, with no warning, they drew their weapon-sticks and chased us away with both shouts and thunder.

Chapter Three: Another Day, Another Dance

I returned to the tribal grounds with my four lieutenants, shaken by what had happened on the hilltop.

I had believed that as dancers, the humans would have to understand the meaning of the sacred wolf-dance. But I had been mistaken, and badly so.

Now, I feared, the men had mistaken my gesture of friendship. Somehow they had misinterpreted it and seen it as an act of hostility, a dance of aggression. Perhaps they thought it was a war-dance.

I wondered how humans might respond to a wolf's war-dance, and I was suddenly seized by a deep, powerful fear for the safety of my tribe, my family.

So, without wasting any time, I divided the tribe into war-companies. I did not want to fight, but if the humans came to attack us, I knew we would have no choice but to defend ourselves.

I thought back to Daggerut's warning, but I did my best to put it out of my mind. Whether or not his words were sensible didn't matter to me at that moment. Honor is honor, and a Thonuk who surrenders his territory without a fight is the lowest of the low, the most dishonorable of the dishonorable.

He becomes what we call a quorinx, in wolf-speak. A disgrace. A coward. I would never allow myself to fail my tribe so deeply, to become a quorinx.

I began to mobilize my troops.

I stationed one company at the mouth of the tribal grounds, another two in the woods flanking the grounds, and a final one on a nearby hilltop overlooking our home.

Despite what you must think, wolves are not violent creatures by nature. We hunt other animals when we are hungry, of course, but we do not enjoy it.

We certainly do not enjoy combat either. I know I have said much about wolf warriors and wolf wars, but we fight only out of a sense of duty and honor. It is something that is done grimly, with great seriousness, and never with eager anticipation.

No wolf of any worth would ever dream of entering battle with joy in his heart; to do so would make him almost as low as quorinx, and show him to be devoid of all honor.

We waited for the humans to arrive at our home-grounds for the rest of the day, nerves tensed to the breaking point.

But they did not come.

When night began to fall, we realized, to our relief, that they would not be coming at all. I had been blessedly mistaken. I had not offended the humans, or frightened them—merely confused them. At least, that is what I now decided.

They did not know what to make of my wolf-dance. But perhaps, when we met again, I might be able to make them understand. The humans were clearly intelligent, and I began to feel confident that we would be able to devise some means of communication.

After all, Tagrut had been able to communicate with the thin-legs. And humans were far more intelligent, were they not? I began to entertain a certain degree of cautious optimism.

Assured that the danger had passed, my tribemates and I gave up our posts and returned to the tribal grounds.

"What do you think happened?" Bona asked me. "Why didn't the humans come?"

"I'm not sure," I admitted. "I still find them very odd and difficult to understand."

"Do you think they can be reasoned with?" Bona asked.

"I'm not certain," I said. "But I'm beginning to think that the answer may be yes. They used their weapon-sticks today, true. But they did not try to hurt or kill us. They merely drove us off."

I remembered my failed attempt at communication and was embarrassed for a moment. "I think," I continued, "that they were confused by the Ut-Nizak."

"But their intentions may still be good, you think?" Bona asked me.

"Yes, I do think it's possible," I said. "We've heard so many horror stories from Daggerut and the others. But surely, not all humans can be the same. There is great variety among the wolf tribes. I would not be surprised if there are many different kinds of human as well."

"Some less violent than others?" Bona asked.

"Yes," I replied, "some less violent than others."

The next morning, I set out for the human camp with my lieutenants. I was convinced that this time, my attempts at communication would prove successful. The humans would understand me, and we would all sit down together to learn more about one another.

What a fool I was!

The humans did not understand me at all.

As I capered and growled and pranced, I saw one of the male humans step forward. He was burly, with fur that grew all over the lower part of his face, and he had a weapon-stick slung across his back.

He narrowed his eyes. Dropping to one knee, he began to raise his stick at me. I understood that the gesture was not a friendly one and quickly ceased my dancing.

Then there was a loud boom from the stick, and for a moment I thought a swarm of angry, buzzing hornets had passed close to my head. What horrible thing was inside this weapon-stick of his?

There was no mistaking the humans' reaction this time. They were not confused or frightened. They were full of hate: I could see it in their eyes.

Once again, my lieutenants and I had to flee from the human camp. Our tails drooped in shame as we realized how badly our mission had failed. None of us uttered a word as we made our way back home.

When I returned to my tribal grounds, I lapsed into a moody silence. Even my beloved wife could not draw me out of it. I knew then that all of Daggerut's stories of humans had been tragically true. There was no way to communicate with the humans or to show them that all that wolves desired was to live together in mutual trust and friendship.

I had offered the humans our tribe's most sacred dance and been offered only violence in return. Clearly, my tribe would not be able to share this land with the race of humans for long.

I was right. Things began to move quickly in the months that followed, and the developments were most unwelcome. My spies began to learn some of the human-speak, and they reported to me what they could of the humans' conversations.

The humans who had arrived in the covered wagon decided that they liked our forest. They were settlers and had traveled far from a place to the east, a place that they called New York.

Although they seemed to like the forest, they felt a need to change it so that it would fit their conception of what a forest should be like. They were unable to sleep on the grassy ground like wolves, so they began to cut down the trees. They used the wood from the trees to build huge shelters for themselves, which I later found out they called cabins.

The humans cut down tree after tree. Sometimes they would leave a worn little nub of wood behind, a tiny stump. Other times, they would leave nothing at all.

They put up several cabins, one for each family in their tribe. At night, they went inside their cabins and didn't come out until the sun rose. They seemed to be hiding from the forest and from each other.

This was very strange to me. In a wolf-tribe, all families live together. But apparently, humans do not choose to live in this way.

I wondered if this was part of humanity's distrust of other creatures: an inability to live together in a spirit of harmony and mutual trust. The more I learned about them, the less they resembled the wolf.

The biggest problem with the humans, of course, was that they didn't seem to have any plans to leave. They had seen our home and decided that they liked it. Somehow, they felt entitled to move in. They had certainly not asked for our permission. On the contrary, they now chased us away whenever we came near. It was not the behavior of good neighbors.

I met with my top lieutenants often in those days, and discussed ways in which we could deal with the humans.

"War," said Tagrut, during our final discussion. "There is no other alternative. The behavior of the humans has been boorish and unacceptable. What makes them think they can march into our homeland and seize it for themselves? What's more, they refuse to associate with us and drive us away with weapon-sticks. They can't be allowed to continue this. It simply cannot be tolerated."

"But we cannot win, Tagrut," I said.

"Who needs to win?" he replied. "We simply need to take a stand. Honor demands it."

"There is more to this than honor," I cut in.

Admittedly, I had viewed the situation solely in terms of honor myself a scant few months before. But I had seen what the humans were capable of, and I finally understood the wisdom of Daggerut.

"More than honor, Ankrut?" scoffed Tagrut. "What else is there besides honor?"

"Quite a lot, actually," I replied. "Honor is something to aspire to, certainly. But it may be a luxury that we cannot afford."

"A luxury?" said Tagrut, aghast. "Honor, a luxury?"

"Yes, a luxury," I continued, my tone firm. "Honor is all well and good when a wolf wants to feel proud of his or her bravery. But I'm not willing to sacrifice the lives of my tribemates to live up to some kind of lofty ideal."

"Coward!" snarled Tagrut. "Are we really supposed to follow a leader who would not stand and fight?"

He looked at my other lieutenants. No one said a word. They just stood and stared at Tagrut and me.

I snarled back. "You should watch your mouth when you talk to your Thonuk."

"Thonuk?" shouted Tagrut. "No, I cannot call you by that name anymore. You don't deserve it!"

"Careful," I said. "You should be careful, Tagrut. That sounds like a challenge."

"It is a challenge!" he roared. "How dare you tarnish the good name of this tribe with your dishonorable ways?"

My lips curled back from my teeth. "If you wish to challenge my authority, then don't waste your time talking about it. Issue the challenge, Tagrut."

He nodded fiercely and then went into the short dance that involved turning in a circle twice and bowing his head. Then he spoke the ceremonial words.

"Thonuk-da, Thonuk-ar-doon," he intoned. "Kashir Thonuk d'arpah."

A rough translation would be, "Present Chieftain, Future Chieftain. I challenge your chieftainship before the tribe."

I accepted his challenge. Before any of my other lieutenants could argue with us or pull us apart, we fought. It was a ferocious battle, brief but intense. Tagrut was both younger and stronger, but I was more experienced, the veteran warrior. The advantage was enough to give me victory.

As our tradition demanded, Tagrut now had no choice but to leave the tribe forever. If a wolf challenges the Thonuk and loses, he is banished.

I had won and retained my position. I suppose I should have been relieved, but I was not. Instead, I felt miserable. Tagrut had been my friend; impulsive and bad-tempered, but my friend, nonetheless.

It pained me to see him leave, and I knew it would hurt my popularity with many of the younger wolves of the tribe. Tagrut was well liked, and many wolf-parents had held him up as a role model before their children.

I could feel things slipping out of control more and more. I'd lost one of my right-hand wolves, and the humans were taking over an increasing portion of our domain; nothing seemed to be going as I wanted it to.

I found myself wishing that Tagrut had won, and that I could step down as Thonuk. Let someone else deal with this problem. Let this be someone else's headache.

What could I do? We could not fight the humans, this was clear. But could we simply leave our home without a fight?

For the first time in my many years as Thonuk, I felt completely useless. The world was changing fast, and I did not know if I would be able to keep up with it. I feared that I would not.

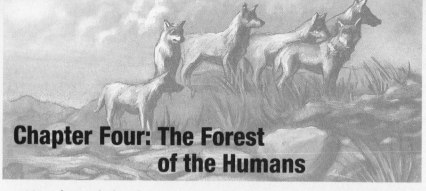

Chapter Four: The Forest of the Humans

We shared the forest with the humans for about ten of your human-months. But everyone in the tribe realized that this sharing would not last. Even the youngest wolves in the pack understood that it would soon be time for us to leave.

I had decided that my only choice was to take the course of action that would ensure the continued survival of my tribe. In this case, that meant doing the thing that I least wanted to do. It meant abandoning our home and fleeing from the humans.

Humans had made it clear that they had no place in their lives for wolves. They would not share their food with us, talk with us, or dance with us. When we appeared, female humans shrieked, and the males chased us away with their awful weapon-sticks.

The Great Forest had been our home for as long as I could remember. It had been the home of our parents, our grandparents, and our great-grandparents. But we all understood that the times were changing. The forest no longer belonged to wolves, but to humans. How could we compete? The ways of the wolf are simple: We hunt, we forage, we dance, and we raise our families.

But humans make everything so complicated. They cut down the trees to make their homes. They tear up the earth to plant their gardens.

Like us, they hunt. But they take much more than they need. With humans around there would never be enough food left in the forest for us.

Once, I had so many fine and lofty ideas. I had wanted to befriend the humans. I had wanted to learn their language and teach them ours. I had wanted to learn their secrets of fire and gardening. I now realized that none of this would come to pass.

We all knew, deep within ourselves, that soon we would have to leave our home. The only thing we did not know was how soon. We hoped that we had at least another year before the humans drove us out.

Unfortunately, we had far less than a year left. After the tenth month of sharing the forest, the humans began to seek us out. They came to the tribal grounds, caught us by surprise, and fired their weapon-sticks at us.

Some of us were hurt. The rest fled into the forest, deep into the tangled bushes, where the humans could not, or would not, follow.

We knew then, without a doubt, that it was over. I felt a great sadness to be giving up the only home I had ever known.

But at the same time, I was not entirely without hope. We would be leaving, yes, but we would find a new home far away from the race of humans. It would take time to adjust to this new home. It always takes time to adapt.

But before we arrived at our new home, we would have to embark upon a great journey. I had heard tales of other wolves that had gone on great journeys, and I realized, to my excitement, that journeys invariably led to adventures.

I had never experienced an adventure before. I had always been too busy protecting my family and my tribe to embark upon a journey of my own, but this would be my chance!

It would be the best kind of journey too. Everyone I cared about would be traveling with me. My wife, my friends, and all seven of my beloved children would come with me.

We had now reached that critical moment. The humans had lost their patience and would no longer tolerate our presence. And surely, as Daggerut had warned me long ago, it would be madness to take a stand against the forces of humanity again.

And so, the next day we set out. We left behind the Great Forest, which we now called by a new name: the Forest of the Humans. And we traveled for many, many human-months.

We encountered other humans along the way, of course, but we now knew better than to approach them. We spied on them from a distance, though, and slowly but surely, I began to learn the human language.

As we continued to travel west, I found that I was even able to begin piecing together bits of human history and culture.

The more I eavesdropped, the more I learned. I learned about great colonies of humans called cities. I also learned about their government, which included a leader called a President, as well as a series of council members they called congressmen.

Perhaps humans were not so different from us after all, I realized. In truth, what was the difference between a President and a Thonuk? Or between a congress and a wolf-council? It was the same idea, just different words, I decided. They were not really such bad creatures, these humans, as it turned out.

After all, they wanted exactly what we wanted: a place to call their home. As I listened to them speak, I heard them talk a great deal about it. It just so happened that the humans had a different way of making a home than we wolves did.

Although we could understand them, we could not make them understand us. If only wolves could speak words like the humans do. But try as we might, all we can manage are yips and howls.

So the barrier between wolfkind and humankind remains. I have spent many years trying to devise a way for wolves to speak the human language. But I have been unsuccessful. It is, I fear, the mission of a fool. But for some reason, I cannot give up on the idea that some day wolves and humans might be able to talk to one another, somehow.

We finally found a new home, I should tell you. We call it "Ozaka-Jokar," which literally means, "The New Place."

It is located in another forest, not far from a cliff that looks out over the crashing waves of Mother Ocean. It is not as nice as our old home, but still it is a pleasant enough place. The air is cool and fresh, and there are many places to hunt and forage.

The road to Ozaka-Jokar was a long one. It took many human-months, perhaps even a year, to get there.

It was a difficult road as well. Disease, starvation, and a lack of clean water plagued us. We were sometimes attacked by other animals, such as mountain lions and bears.

We were even, on one occasion, attacked by a renegade tribe of wolves. My tribe was able to fend them off, of course, but our losses were great. I was shocked at the time (and am still dismayed today) to realize that even in the face of as powerful an antagonist as humans, some wolves still refuse to band together for the common good.

I suppose, in that way, we are not so very different from the humans after all. We can be just as selfish as I have taken humans to be.

We pressed on, and we endured many hardships, much pain, and much suffering. Ultimately, our persistence was rewarded, and we stumbled upon Ozaka-Jokar.

Many years have passed since that day when the humans first came into our forest. I am old now. I am no longer leader of the tribe. That role has been inherited by Fona, my eldest daughter.

She has made a very worthy Thonuk, I am proud to say. She is strong, but not proud; honorable, but never haughty. She is, in short, everything that a good leader should be. The tribe respects and admires her, and they would follow her just about anywhere.

It is a relief to me. A good leader is more important than almost anything when it comes to the well-being of a tribe.

I am fortunate in my old age. I still have my good health. I still have my loving and devoted wife, Bona. I have countless grandchildren and great-grandchildren who bring me great joy in my declining years.

I have had, in all honesty, a good life for a wolf. You may have trouble believing that, for there has been much sadness, much uncertainty in my days. I was attacked by humans anxious to steal my forest and lost my home to them. I have traveled far and seen many things I would rather not have seen.

But still, there is much in my life I can be proud of. I believe now more than ever that I made the right decision. Honor is important, but the safety of my tribe had to come first.

There have been regrets, of course. There is one, in particular, that stands out from the pack.

I have always regretted that no matter how hard I tried, I could not teach the humans the beauty of the Ut-Nizak, the wolf-dance of friendship and welcome.

Settlers and the Oregon Trail

During the 1800s the lure of wide open spaces drove many people out of the crowded cities of the East to the unsettled western frontier. Many of the first pioneers who traveled to the Oregon Territory were French Canadians, eager to make a living as fur traders. However, as the years passed, more and more United States residents began to join them, embarking upon the long journey to Oregon.

Many settlers traveled to Oregon by wagon train during the 1840s, taking a route that became known as the Oregon Trail. By 1847 more than five thousand settlers traveled on the trail each year. Until the 1860s it was the chief passage across the country.

Many of the settlers didn't follow the trail all the way to Oregon. They settled along the way in places such as present-day Idaho or left the trail to settle in Nevada, California, or Utah.

The Oregon Trail covered roughly two thousand miles and was physically demanding. Most pioneers relied on strong, sturdy beasts such as mules and oxen to pull their covered wagons. However, many pioneers traveled on foot. Some of these determined settlers didn't have shoes to wear and walked barefoot!

A pioneer camp on the Oregon Trail in Nebraska